①45

Journey to Freedom

SOJOURNER TRUTH

BY LAURA SPINALE

"CHILDREN, WHO MADE YOUR SKIN WHITE? WAS IT NOT GOD? WHO MADE MINE BLACK? WAS IT NOT THE SAME GOD? AM I TO BLAME, THEREFORE, BECAUSE MY SKIN IS BLACK?"

— SOJOURNER TRUTH

Cover and page 4 caption:
Sojourner Truth in 1864

Content Consultant:
Mary Butler, director of the
Research Center, Sojourner
Truth Institute

Published in the United States of America by The Child's World®
1980 Lookout Drive, Mankato, MN 56003-1705
800-599-READ • www.childsworld.com

ACKNOWLEDGEMENTS

The Child's World®: Mary Berendes, Publishing Director

The Design Lab: Kathleen Petelinsek, Design; Gregory Lindholm, Page Production

Red Line Editorial: Holly Saari, Editorial Direction

PHOTOS

Cover and page 4: Library of Congress

Interior: Amelia P. Lincoln/AP Images, 5; Library of Congress, 6, 11, 13, 16, 18, 23, 25; Corbis, 7; Nik Wheeler/Corbis, 8; North Wind Picture Archives, 9, 12, 19; North Wind Picture Archives/ Photo Library, 17; AP Images, 21, 22, 24, 26; Dennis Macdonald/Photo Library, 27

LIBRARY OF CONGRESS CATALOGING-IN-PUBLICATION DATA

Spinale, Laura, 1966–

  Sojourner Truth / by Laura Spinale.

    p. cm. — (Journey to freedom)

  Includes bibliographical references and index.

  ISBN 978-1-60253-135-2 (library bound : alk. paper)

  1. Truth, Sojourner, d. 1883——Juvenile literature 2. African American abolitionists— Biography—Juvenile literature. 3. African American women—Biography—Juvenile literature. 4. Abolitionists—United States—Biography—Juvenile literature. 5. Social reformers—United States—Biography—Juvenile literature. I. Title. II. Series.

  E185.97.T8S656 2009

  306.3'62092—dc22

  [B]

                                 2009003652

CONTENTS

Sometimes slave masters made slaves beat or whip other slaves.

Chapter Two

A LIFE IN CAPTIVITY

Slavery in the United States began with the first colonies in the 1600s. Slaves were forced to work for wealthier people and were often treated cruelly. Their masters, or owners, often beat them. Slaves worked many hours and received no pay in return. Their lives were extremely difficult.

Isabella was born into slavery in New York around 1797. She never knew the exact year of her birth. Most slave owners did not keep records of the births or deaths of their slaves. Isabella's parents, James and Betsey, were both slaves. The Hardenbergh family owned them.

Johannis Hardenbergh was said to have treated his slaves fairly well. Still, Isabella and her family did not have an easy life. They lived in a small, underground cellar with only one tiny window. Even during the day, the room was almost completely dark. The family slept on wooden boards placed on the cold, damp floor. Water dripped through cracks in the walls when it rained. Sometimes, the ground turned into a big pool of mud.

Isabella was never really sure how many brothers and sisters she had. She never knew most of them. Hardenbergh sold most of her brothers and sisters to other families before Isabella was born. Isabella only knew her younger brother, Peter.

Former slave quarters in South Carolina

8

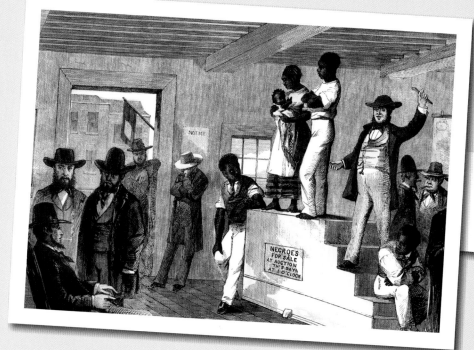

A family on the auction block, about to be separated and sold into slavery

Betsey, Isabella's mother, was a **Christian**. She taught Isabella and Peter to pray. Betsey believed that only God could help her family survive. Praying comforted Isabella. It made her feel as though someone was watching over her. Betsey also told Isabella how important it was to obey her owners. She promised Isabella that if she was very good, she would be rewarded someday.

Unfortunately, Isabella was soon separated from her family. When she was about 9 years old, Hardenbergh died. His family sold his belongings, including his slaves. James and Betsey were too old to sell. The Hardenbergh family decided to set them free. They let them stay in the cold, dark, cellar room. However, Isabella was sold to the Neely family for $100.

Slaves were considered their masters' property. They were bought and sold at auctions similar to how paintings and other items are bought and sold at auctions today.

Up to this point, Isabella only spoke the Dutch language. (The Hardenberghs were Dutch.) Isabella had never heard English until she was sold to the Neely family. She could not speak a word of English when she first arrived. When the Neelys asked her to do something, she could not understand them. Isabella's new owners were cruel to her. They believed she was disobedient or stupid because she could not understand them. John Neely often beat her.

When Isabella learned that her mother had died, she asked for permission to visit her father, James. During this visit, James learned that Neely beat Isabella. James knew that something should be done. He asked a fisherman named Martinus Schryver to buy Isabella. Schryver was a kinder master than Neely.

After about one year, Schryver sold Isabella to the Dumont family. Isabella had a difficult time with her new owners. John Dumont occasionally beat her, although not as harshly as Neely had. Dumont's wife did not like Isabella and made her life very difficult. Mrs. Dumont often blamed Isabella for mistakes that other workers had made.

However, Dumont recognized that Isabella was an excellent worker. She could work long and hard. In the mornings, she worked in the fields. At night, she cleaned and did laundry. Dumont said Isabella could do as much farm work as his best male slaves.

While working for Dumont, Isabella met a young slave named Robert. He lived on a nearby farm.

This woodcut, created around 1834, shows a female master whipping her slave girl.

Robert came to visit Isabella whenever he could. The two made secret plans to marry. When Robert's master found out, he became angry. He told Robert to stop seeing Isabella. The master wanted Robert to marry one of his slaves. But Robert and Isabella continued to meet in secret.

Robert's master soon found out. The next time Robert went to visit Isabella, his master followed him and brutally beat him. Robert finally agreed to marry one of the master's slaves. Isabella never saw him again.

Isabella was forced to marry one of Dumont's slaves named Thomas. She did not love him, but Isabella had to obey her master. Isabella's first child was born in 1815. She and Thomas had several more children together. Isabella taught all of them to be obedient and honest, just as her mother had taught her. For many years, Isabella continued to work hard for the Dumont family.

Two slaves getting married

Chapter Three

FREEDOM FOUND

I n 1817, New York passed a law that freed slaves in the state who were born before 1799. Since Isabella was born before 1799, she would be freed. These slaves would be freed on July 4, 1827. However, Dumont and Isabella came to an agreement that he would free her early because of her hard work.

Isabella tried to do everything the Dumont family asked of her. She worked as hard as she could so she could be freed earlier. In 1825, she cut her hand as she worked in the fields. It was a serious injury. For many months, she could not work as hard as she had before.

In 1826, Isabella asked Dumont to set her free as he said he would. He refused. Dumont said that Isabella owed him another year because she had not worked very hard while her hand was injured. Isabella disagreed with Dumont. She believed her hard work throughout all her years with Dumont was enough to keep her end of the agreement. She decided to leave. One morning in late 1826, Isabella woke before dawn and walked away from the Dumonts' property. She carried her youngest daughter, Sophia, with her.

Isabella was now an escaped slave. She had no money or food. Sophia was still a baby and needed care. Isabella first stopped at the house of Levi Rowe, who was an old friend. He could not help her because he was very sick, but he directed her to the house of the Van Wagenen family. Isabella had known them for some time. They and the Dumonts were members of the same church. Unlike the Dumonts, however, the Van Wagenens were against slavery. The Van Wagenens were kind to Isabella. She was not used to this. All her life, Isabella had been told that blacks were **inferior** to whites. Sometimes, she even believed it. Isabella could not believe that she was finally being treated as an equal.

Soon, Dumont learned where Isabella was. He tried to force Isabella to return. The Van Wagenens had to pay Dumont for both Isabella and Sophia. They paid $20 for Isabella and $5 for Sophia. The Van Wagenens then set them free.

Now free, Isabella began to gain self-respect. She found a job as a seamstress and then as a maid.

The Van Wagenen family gave Isabella a room in which to sleep. It was the first time she ever slept in a bed.

For the first time, people paid her for the work she did. Now that she was free, she wanted no part of her former life as a slave. She took the last name of the kind family who had helped her. She became known as Isabella Van Wagenen.

The New York law did not free all the state's slaves at once. The younger slaves had to remain with their masters until they reached their twenties. Isabella had several children. Every one of them, except Sophia, still belonged to Dumont. Isabella had left them behind to gain her own freedom.

In late 1826, Isabella learned that her son, Peter, was gone. The Dumonts had given him to a relative, Solomon Gedney, who took Peter to the South. Isabella was furious. She knew that the Dumonts had broken the law. It was illegal for slaves in New York to be sent to the South. They had to stay in the North until they were set free. If Peter was forced to stay in the South, he might be a slave forever. Isabella could not bear this. She decided to face the Dumonts.

Dumont said he had not known that Gedney would take Peter to the South. He even felt sorry for Isabella. But Mrs. Dumont laughed at her former slave. She thought it was foolish to be so upset about a black child. To her, Peter was no different than any other property. But Isabella wanted her child back.

With her friends' help, Isabella sued the Dumonts in order to get Peter back. No one believed that she

Isabella filed and won three lawsuits in her life. The first was to get back her son, Peter. The second time, she sued members of a religious community for talking badly about her. The third time, she sued a Washington DC streetcar conductor who would not let her ride the car and tried to force her out.

could win a case against a rich, white family. The fact that Isabella, as a former slave and a black woman, felt she should be able to use the justice system showed her courage. It also showed her strong sense of right and wrong.

During the trial in 1828, Isabella's **lawyer** told Peter's story before a judge. He told the judge how poorly Peter had been treated. Gedney had beaten him. Peter's back, forehead, and cheek were covered with scars. The judge saw that Peter was very frightened. He decided Gedney could not keep Peter. Isabella won her case.

A courtroom scene in Washington DC in the mid-1800s

A black woman working as a servant for a white woman

Isabella's belief in God had continued to grow during her fight for Peter. She now believed that God was responsible for her success. Isabella decided to learn more about her religion. She also decided to go to New York City. She knew she could find a better job there. Perhaps one day, she could buy a small house where all her children could live.

In 1828, Isabella and Peter arrived in New York City. Sadly, she had to leave Sophia with her other children at the Dumonts' home. It would be too difficult to work long hours with such young children. Once in New York City, Isabella found work as a maid.

In New York City, Isabella's son, Peter, became a bit of a troublemaker. In 1839, when he was 18, Isabella made Peter join a whaling ship. She hoped that once he was away from the temptations of New York, he would straighten out. After Peter left for sea, Isabella received a few letters, but she never saw him again.

Truth preached at prayer gatherings.

Chapter Four

ON THE ROAD

n 1843, Isabella believed that God appeared to her in a dream. God told her to deliver the messages of the **Gospel** across the land. Isabella gathered the few belongings she had and left the city with just 25 cents. She felt she should change her name again. Isabella was the name she had during her years as a slave. She did not want it any longer. Isabella was going to sojourn, or travel, to preach the messages of the Gospel. So she changed her name to Sojourner Truth.

Eventually Truth came to a Massachusetts community called Northampton. Members of the community owned and operated a silk mill. They also believed in social equality. They thought people of different skin colors, genders, and religions should all be treated equally. Truth came to think of this community as her home. She said she was allowed "equality of feeling" and "liberty of thought and speech."

While in Northampton, Truth first met abolitionists. She learned that the antislavery message the abolitionists preached could be woven into her speeches. When Truth left Northampton, she began including an antislavery message in her preaching. Truth traveled from town to town throughout the Northern states to preach the word of God and to speak out against slavery. She went as far west as Missouri and Kansas preaching her message of equality and faith. Many people respected her ideas. They invited her to stay in their homes.

A black worship service

Sojourner Truth captured the attention of her audiences. She was six feet tall and wore a white turban on her head. She carried herself with great pride. She had large muscles from years of hard work. But it was not just her appearance that struck people. Truth's thoughts and ideas impressed many who listened. Her audiences found truth in her arguments against slavery. People listened to her wherever she went.

During that time in the United States, free women did not have the same rights as men. They were considered second-class citizens. Women in the United States were not allowed to vote. **Suffragists** hoped to change this. They worked for a woman's right to vote.

In 1850, Truth joined the women's rights movement and became a suffragist. She believed every U.S. citizen deserved the same rights. In 1851, Truth gave her famous "Ain't I a Woman?" speech to the Women's Rights Convention in Ohio.

Things were not always easy for Truth. Some abolitionists refused to let her join them because she was a woman. Some suffragists refused her because she was black. Even with these setbacks, Truth kept working for equality.

In 1857, she decided to settle in the town of Battle Creek, Michigan. Many abolitionists lived in this area. Truth joined a religious group and made several new friends. She was 60 years old and wanted a place to

*Like most former slaves, Truth was **illiterate**. She had never been taught to read or write. Yet, even without schooling, she was a smart woman.*

This wood engraving shows an 1880 meeting of a women's rights group.

call home. Later, some of her children moved to Battle Creek to be close to her.

Truth continued to travel and to give speeches. The country was in the midst of a difficult time. Abolitionists were speaking out against slavery more firmly than ever. But the South still did not want to lose the free labor of enslaved workers.

By January of 1861, several Southern states **seceded** from the **Union**. More states followed and the **Confederate States of America** was formed. President Abraham Lincoln would not allow the Confederate states to secede from the Union. On April 12, 1861, the U.S. Civil War began.

In January of 1863, the Emancipation Proclamation freed all the slaves living in the Confederate states. But Southerners living there did not consider themselves to be part of the United States. They did not feel they had to follow the president's orders. They refused to free their slaves. Millions of slaves continued to work just as they always had.

Sojourner Truth continued to speak out during the war. More and more people came to hear her preach. President Lincoln invited her to the White House. The president respected Truth's views. After her visit, Truth said, "I must say, and I am proud to say, that I never was treated by anyone with more kindness and cordiality than were shown to me by that great and good man, Abraham Lincoln."

A copy of the Emancipation Proclamation

The war between the Northern and Southern states continued into 1865. The South finally surrendered on April 9, 1865. In December of 1865, Congress passed the Thirteenth **Amendment**. This act formally freed all slaves in the United States. But Truth understood that freedom and equality were two different things. There was still much work to be done.

This painting, created around 1893, portrays Abraham Lincoln and Sojourner Truth's meeting.

Sojourner Truth
in 1864

Chapter Five

AFTER THE WAR

nfortunately, once slaves were freed, whites still did not treat them well. Many people continued to believe that blacks were inferior. Sojourner Truth still had work to do—both for blacks and for women. The government **appointed** Truth to the Federal Freedman's Bureau. This organization helped former slaves start their lives as free men and women. Truth helped these former slaves find land and homes. She worked on fighting black poverty.

Truth helped black women learn skills to help them find jobs. In 1868, the Fourteenth Amendment granted black men the right to vote. Truth knew this was a big step, but women of any color still did not have the right to vote. She continued to work with the suffragists. In 1872, Truth tried to cast a vote in the presidential election. Workers blocked her entrance to the voting booth.

Truth continued to speak in public, but over time, she became ill. She died in Battle Creek in 1883. Truth had not been afraid of death. She believed that God would be with her after she died.

Approximately 1,000 people attended Sojourner Truth's funeral. A well-known abolitionist and suffragist spoke to the crowd. He told everyone about the remarkable woman named Sojourner Truth.

Truth was one of the first black women to fight for slaves' freedom. She was also among the first black women to fight for a woman's right to vote. Her accomplishments were not always recognized during her lifetime. Nor were her speeches and beliefs always liked. Once when Truth was preparing to speak in Indiana, someone told her that if she was going to speak there, the building would be burned down. Truth replied, "Then I will speak upon the ashes." Her commitment to social equality never weakened.

Women were granted the right to vote in 1920 when the Nineteenth Amendment to the U.S. Constitution was passed.

Women casting their votes in New York around 1920

Sojourner Truth
22

Black Heritage USA

The 1986 postage stamp
honoring Sojourner Truth

Today many people have honored Sojourner Truth's name. She is now considered by many to be one of the most important black women of the nineteenth century, along with Harriet Ross Tubman. In 1986, the U.S. Postal Service designed a postage stamp with Truth's picture. In 1997, NASA launched a probe to study Mars. That probe was named *Sojourner* in honor of Sojourner Truth.

Truth knew that even after the Civil War, the journey to freedom would not come easily or quickly for blacks. She knew that any social reform took time and commitment. Her strong Christian faith inspired her to continue to speak about equality throughout her life.

A statue of Sojourner Truth in Battle Creek, Michigan

TIME LINE

1790   **1820**   **1840**   **1850**

CA. 1797
Isabella is born into slavery in New York.

1826
Isabella escapes from the Dumonts with her daughter, Sophia.

1828
Isabella and her son, Peter, move to New York City.

1843
Isabella believes God appears to her. She changes her name to Sojourner Truth.

1850
Truth becomes involved in the women's rights movement.

1851
Truth gives her "Ain't I a Woman?" speech at the Women's Rights Convention in Akron, Ohio.

1861
The U.S. Civil War begins.

1865
Congress passes the Thirteenth Amendment, which frees all slaves in the United States.

1872
Truth tries to vote in a presidential election but is blocked from doing so.

1883
Truth dies in Battle Creek, Michigan, in her mid-eighties.

1986
The U.S. Postal Service releases a Sojourner Truth postage stamp.

1997
NASA launches the *Sojourner* probe to study Mars; it is named to honor Sojourner Truth.

GLOSSARY

abolitionist
(*ab-uh-**lish**-uh-nist*)
An abolitionist was a person who worked to end slavery. Truth became an abolitionist after she was freed from slavery.

amendment
(*uh-**mend**-munt*)
An amendment is a change that is made to a law or legal document. The Thirteenth Amendment to the U.S. Constitution ended slavery in the United States.

appointed
(*uh-**poyn**-ted*)
If someone is appointed, he or she is selected for a job. The government appointed Truth to the Federal Freedman's Bureau.

Christian
(***kriss**-chin*)
A Christian is a person whose religion is based on the life and teachings of Jesus Christ. Truth was a Christian.

Confederate States of America
(*kun-**fed**-ur-ut **states of** uh-**mayr**-uh-kuh*)
The Confederate States of America were the Southern states that withdrew from the United States during the U.S. Civil War. The Confederate States of America formed after those states seceded from the Union.

dialect
(***dy**-uh-lekt*)
A dialect is a way language is spoken in an area or by a group of people. Frances Gage's account of Truth's "Ain't I a Woman?" speech used black dialect.

Gospel
(***goss**-pull*)
The Gospel consists of the books of the Bible that describe the teachings and life of Jesus Christ. Truth preached the Gospel.

illiterate
(*il-**it**-ur-it*)
If people are illiterate, they cannot read or write. Truth was illiterate.

inferior
(*in-**feer**-ee-ur*)
If something is inferior, it is not as good as something else. Blacks were often made to feel inferior to whites.

lawyer
(***loy**-ur*)
A lawyer is a person who advises others about the law and speaks for them in court. Truth hired a lawyer when she wanted to get back her son, Peter.

plantations
(*plan-**tay**-shunz*)
Plantations were large farms that were usually in the South. Slaves often worked on plantations.

seceded
(*si-**see**-ded*)
If something or someone formally withdraws from a group, it has seceded. The Southern states seceded from the Union before the Civil War began.

suffragists
(***suf**-ru-jists*)
Suffragists were women and men who worked for women's right to vote. Truth was an outspoken suffragist.

Union
(***yoon**-yun*)
The Union refers to the states that stayed loyal to the U.S. government during the U.S. Civil War. The Union army fought against the Confederate army in the war.

FURTHER INFORMATION

Books

Carey, Charles W. Jr. *The Emancipation Proclamation.* Mankato, MN: Child's World, 2009.

Kamma, Anne. . . . *If You Lived When Women Won Their Rights.* New York: Scholastic, 2008.

Landau, Elaine. *Women's Right to Vote.* New York: Children's Press, 2007.

Rossi, Ann. *Freedom Struggle: The Anti-Slavery Movement 1830–1865.* Des Moines, IA: National Geographic School Publishing, 2005.

Truth, Sojourner. Margaret Washington, ed. *Narrative of Sojourner Truth.* New York: Knopf, 1993.

Videos

Life of Sojourner Truth: Ain't I a Woman? Phoenix Learning Group, 2008.

One Woman, One Vote. PBS, 2006.

Web Sites

Visit our Web page for links about Sojourner Truth:

http://www.childsworld.com/links

NOTE TO PARENTS, TEACHERS, AND LIBRARIANS: We routinely verify our Web links to make sure they are safe, active sites—so encourage your readers to check them out!

Index